The 5 Secrets To Making A POWERFUL Business Presentation

by Carl Henry

Book design by Nichole Ward, Morrison Alley Design

First Printing 2010

ISBN-13 978-0-9817915-4-8

For Will and Virginia

Contents

When you stand up

to present to a group,

you sit down a little bit stronger.

CHAPTER ONE

Bringing Your Business Presentations to Life

When I was a kid, playing baseball meant grabbing a glove, heading outside, and pretending to be one of my favorite players. It took a lot of imagination, but if I pictured it just right, I could be at home plate in Yankee Stadium staring down the opposing pitcher in the ninth. These days, a young person is never farther away than their high-definition television from practically being their favorite sports star – a complete digital representation, including their movements, voice, and a virtual atmosphere that looks and sounds almost as good as the real thing.

Before you get concerned that I'm going to start into an essay about how easy today's kids have it, let me just say that, if anything, I'm jealous. If we would have had those kinds of games when I was a kid, I certainly would have played them, too. Sadly, we didn't. It's taken various forms of technology – ideas that were little more than dreams when I was young – decades to even begin to catch up to our imaginations.

To those of us outside the videogame industry, each new development can seem smooth and seamless; every year it seems like our kids are playing games that run just a little bit faster and smoother. If you were to take a look behind the curtain, however, you'd find that an enormous amount of work goes into every title that's released. Not only are there entire teams of developers and animators hard at work, but also actors, writers, sound technicians, and dozens of other creative and computer professionals, all striving to produce a product that feels almost as sharp as real life.

And it works. Just look at any teenager absorbed in his or her favorite game, and you'll see that they aren't just playing it – they're *immersed* in it. All the hard work that went into producing the title is successful simply because you don't notice most of it. It wouldn't be as much fun if you had to pay attention to all the behind-the-scenes coding and effort, so they get you to focus on the great music and visuals.

This is the same force that's at work when you lose yourself in a good book, movie, or live performance. The actors, writers, or production crews have removed every obstacle that could inhibit your absorbing the entertainment; all you have to do is sit back and enjoy.

What does any of this have to do with your business presentations? A lot more than you might think. The same principles that make movie studios, book publishers, and videogame companies millions of dollars can do wonders for your career and reputation. That's because a good speech is as much entertainment as it is information; it's not just about what you say, but whether or not you let people take it in without noticing how hard you're trying to get them to. Put another way, the best presenters aren't giving presentations – they are master storytellers who use showmanship to reinforce their point.

To use these tools effectively, you're going to have to learn something that I call *business choreography*. If those two words seem odd together, don't fret – I'm not going to ask you to break into a dance routine as a way to increase your productivity. What I *am* going to suggest, however, is that the average professional can help his or her career monumentally by learning a few basic concepts from the performing arts.

Here's why: in order to get ahead in today's world, it is an absolute necessity that you become comfortable working with groups. If you can't deliver an effective sales presentation, for example, or speak to your board of directors with authority, then you are placing a strict limit on how far you can advance – not to mention how much money you can make.

Chances are this is something you've heard and understand already. Being a strong public speaker is a natural sign of leadership, and those who can deliver their advice and opinions to groups of people almost always stand out above their peers. What's more, time has only made this skill more important. Ever-increasing numbers of corporations and associations are turning to committees to make the most important decisions. If you want to make a big sale, start a high-level relationship, or get the big promotion, you're going to have to get in front of a few strangers and make a strong impression.

So what holds people back from becoming great presenters and enjoying all of these benefits to their career? I suspect it has to do with a common misconception, and one I hear all the time: that all great speakers are born with some extraordinary talent, and that if you're not a naturally theatrical person, it's just not going to work for you.

I can understand where people get this idea; it's certainly true that some of us take to public speaking a lot more easily than others. And yet, having worked as a professional speaker myself for more than two decades – and seeing countless others come up in the industry during that time – I can tell you without a doubt that speaking is a skill you can learn, and that even the most naturally talented presenter will have to work at it continually if he or she is going to become better than average.

Most of that work, though, consists of having the right mindset. That's because great presentations aren't about having the right slides to display, or putting on the right suit; it's in understanding that every time you get up to speak to a group, you have to put on a show.

That's where the *choreography* part of the process comes in. When people go to see a great live performance of any kind, whether it's at a comedy club, performing arts center, or some other venue, they know in the back of their minds that the show or routine they're seeing has been practiced countless times over. And yet, the very best performers make it look effortless and spontaneous. They've become so attuned to delivering their lines and movements to perfection that you don't notice anything but the show.

Can the same be said about most of the business presentations you see? I doubt it. Most of the speakers I come across, including quite a few professionals, lack the elements of showmanship in their speeches. But you can't educate or persuade until you first excite and entertain. There's a reason the television commercials we all see so often feature crazy music, funny lines, and even cartoon characters running across the screen – and it isn't that advertisers want to be sure you're having a good time. They know that if they want to interest you in their products, they have to interest you in watching the commercial first.

Luckily, building a compelling presentation isn't nearly as hard as you might think. In fact, you have an enormous advantage over our friends in the advertising business, because they have to try to catch your attention at a time when you could just get up and walk away, or simply change the channel, at any given moment. During a live talk, however, most audiences are only going to be a few feet from you. You don't have to perform back flips to keep them from nodding off; you just have to know a few basic skills and work them effectively.

Over the next several pages, I'm going to show you how to do exactly that. I'm not only going to teach you how to grab an audience, bring them around to your point of view, and magnify your career prospects at the same time – but how to have fun while you're doing it.

Giving powerful presentations is a must for anyone who wants to be a leader or top performer. But first, you have to know the four basic elements of any good speech.

Great Presenters

don't just win you over with topics;

they keep you on the

edge of your seat with showmanship.

CHAPTER TWO

The Four Elements of a Good Presentation

What makes for a strong presentation? Most people, if pressed, would probably answer that a strong topic was important, or that lots of preparation was the key. Certainly, those things matter, but neither one is enough to make you effective. We've all heard speeches on interesting topics that somehow fell flat, and well-prepared keynotes that left us wondering where the nearest exits were. So, as important as topics and preparation are to the success of your presentation, you'll need something else if you're going to hold an audience's attention.

The search for that "something else" took me several years, beginning with my first sales presentations in upstate New York, and continuing through my time as a Certified Speaking Professional with the National Speakers Association.

What I found is that presenting is a skill, just like driving or playing the piano. We're all born with some level of natural talent, but all of us – from the best to the worst – can improve significantly by practicing some basic techniques that I first learned long ago. Through years of studying some of the greatest public speakers, people like John F. Kennedy and Martin Luther King, I noticed that almost every good presentation had four elements:

Stories. People love stories – whether it's telling them, hearing them, or passing them on. They take the experiences of our lives and turn them into memorable blocks that we can remember and learn from. They also add smoothness to your presentation and make the points easier to remember.

Usually, when I point this out, it isn't too long before someone asks where they should look for good stories to use in their presentations. The first place I would advise you to look would be within your own personal experiences. Think about your speech topic, and how it relates to you. Was there a time when the information you're sharing was a big help to you? Do you know someone who went through what you're trying to describe? We all wish we had more firsthand business knowledge. Showing how the advice or insight you're about to give has transformed someone's career, or company, is a great way to grab attention.

Another place to find good stories is books or magazines. A quick look through your professional library might lead you to dozens of stories that would be relevant to your target audience or industry. You could also look for similar material online, although it goes without saying that not everything you find on the Internet is going to be trustworthy or useful.

And finally, if you can't find the kind of story you're looking for, why not seek out someone who could tell you one? If your topic is popular enough to draw an audience for a speech, then there must be dozens of other authorities and personalities with the right kind of experience. Providing they aren't speaking at the same event you are, the chances are very good that one of these folks would be happy to share a good story with you.

In fact, the big problem isn't usually in finding stories; it's in deciding which ones to include. If you're not sure about something you want to use, ask yourself a key question: why do I want to tell this story? If it's because it pertains to the issue at hand, or can shed some light on some aspect of your presentation that you'd like to make interesting and memorable, then try it out. If, on the other hand, it's just something you thought was funny or strange, keep looking.

Once you've zeroed in on an anecdote, try to find out exactly what happened and build those details in the way you tell it. The reason stories can connect with us so strongly is that they allow us to put ourselves in another time, place, or other person's shoes. To do that, though, you need to paint a vivid picture. The only way is by giving lots of good details, so practice putting them into your story.

And finally, remember that any story is only as effective as it is relevant. When you've finished telling your audience what happened, bring it back around to the point of your talk. It doesn't matter how funny, emotional, or eye-opening any event was – or how well you told it – if the people listening can't figure out why it matters.

Quotations. No matter what you're trying to say, chances are someone else has gotten to it first and said it better than you can. What's more, people attach more credibility to statements that come from celebrities and historical figures. After all, who would you rather get advice from, Jane Mid-Level Manager or Abe Lincoln? Take advantage of this fact and sprinkle a couple of quotes throughout your presentation.

Don't just quote anybody, however, and don't simply parrot their words. Every quote should have a reason for being in your presentation, and that reason needs to be something stronger than "it fills a few seconds of dead air." Give the quote and the source, but then go on to talk about what it means to you, or why it's relevant to your discussion.

At the same time, realize that not every quote has to be heavy or serious. As sharp and insightful as the writings of Homer and Socrates might have been, quips from others like Mark Twain and George Carlin can often pull out a couple of chuckles while you're making your point. There's nothing wrong with a little levity. In fact, as I've gotten older, I've often taken to quoting myself. Why not? It's all in good fun, and it shows my audience that I'm not taking myself too seriously. I'm not suggesting that talking about yourself in the third person is a surefire way to build a great presentation, of course, but that it's all right to look past Ghandi and George Washington for inspiration.

Famous quotations help your presentation by allowing you to frame ideas differently, and they add to your credibility. As with any keys to an effective presentation, you need to be careful that you don't use them too much – after all, it's still your presentation – but if you find in your research that someone famous agrees with what you're saying, why not bring it up?

Statistics. We've all learned that "the numbers don't lie," so be sure to use them when making your case. Not only will it make your presentation seem better-researched, it will make it more convincing as well. Would you believe that 90 percent of us respond to numerical data? (I made that last one up, but it's a good example of the way statistics work.)

Besides, of all the tools you can use to spice up your presentation and give it more weight, statistics are among the easiest to find. We live in a culture that's seemingly obsessed – and sometimes overrun – with percentages and figures. Corporate groups, consultants, universities, and especially the government, all produce their own statistics on a regular basis. Finding them is as easy as going online or spending fifteen minutes in your local library.

If you want to give your presentation an extra kick, come up with your own statistics. To be clear, I'm absolutely not suggesting that you invent a set of numbers to support your cause or argument (in fact, I seem to recall that a few accountants have gotten into trouble for that in recent years.) Instead, what I'm recommending is that you survey your audience, or a group of their peers. You can do this by phone, e-mail, or a quick in-person survey. Those of you who have been to my seminars already know that I like to ask questions and take short polls. What do I do with that data? I use it for material that helps me make an immediate point, or keep it as an interesting number for a future speech.

Regardless of where you find your statistics, the important thing is that they be accurate, and that they somehow build toward a point or argument you are trying to make. Being armed with a few compelling numbers and percentages gives your message a lot more impact, so do what you can to include them in your presentation.

Humor. You need to use humor in your presentation for the same reason that children's medicine is supposed to taste like bubble gum – it makes the tougher stuff easier to swallow. We all like to be entertained, and adding a few laughs is a great way to keep things moving. A couple words of caution, though: first, don't overdo it. If you're naturally funny, use that talent to deliver your point. But you don't want to let your presentation degrade into an open-mike night.

Second, use the humor that's available to you. If you aren't great at writing jokes, it's all right to borrow some humor from somewhere else. Just don't claim it as your own. It's unethical to do so, and there is a big risk that someone in your audience will recognize the material, at which point all of your credibility will go down the drain. Of course, there is a third option: hiring a professional joke writer. A quick look through your local online listings will probably yield a dozen or more comic writers who are willing to punch up your speech with a couple of laughs. If you have a very important talk coming up, or one that you'll be giving several times, it might be worth the investment.

If you have some time, though, finding humor to throw into your talk is usually pretty easy; you just have to keep your ears open and pay attention to what other people laugh at. For example, I once had a big fear of flying. To help me get over it, a pilot acquaintance of mine offered to let me sit in the cockpit for a short flight. I accepted, and once we were airborne, the pilot showed me how he had planned the route, gotten updates on the weather, and programmed the navigational instruments. After we had gone through all that, I asked where we were actually going. The pilot's answer: "to have this plane fixed."

It's just a small story, and one that usually gets a few laughs, but that's the whole point. You aren't looking to headline at the Laugh Factory; and even if you could, it wouldn't necessarily be great for your presentation, since too much humor can be a distraction. So look for something to break the ice, use it to loosen things up, and then get to the next point.

Because humor is so important to your presentation, I have three final thoughts. First, stick with funny stories and stay away from jokes. The priest and the rabbi who walk into a bar just don't have a place in your business speech. Second, don't use any humor that's going to offend anybody. If you have any doubt at all whether someone in the audience would get upset with what you're saying, don't risk it to get a laugh.

And finally, realize that comedy takes work. Very few people are naturally funny, and the speakers you see who seem like they are have usually taken lots of classes to come off that way. There's no reason you can't do the same. Nearly every urban area has comedy clubs with weekend and evening classes. Give up a few hours and the price of a couple meals out, and you'd be surprised how quickly you can improve your comedy chops. Stick with it, and you might even learn how to pass off jokes and funny stories seamlessly. Make no mistake – the more effortless a joke looks, the more practice went into it. If you're serious about using humor in your presentations, start practicing early and often.

Putting the Pieces Together

Notice that I said most compelling speakers and presenters use these tools, not that they necessarily use *all* of them, or in the same proportions. For some of us, storytelling comes naturally, but humor is hard to master. Others find the laughs easy to deliver, but aren't as comfortable with quotes. The key is to find what works for you and hone it, not to try to imitate what has worked for somebody else.

No matter which ones come naturally to you, try to keep these basics in mind as you prepare and deliver your presentation. Using them won't guarantee you excellent results, but they will give you a strong foundation to start with as you move through the rest of this book.

In the next chapter, I will lead you through The 5 POWER Presentation Steps. Stories, quotes, statistics, and humor are used in powerful presentations, but having them without a system is like having a list of ingredients, but not the recipe.

In order to make your presentations stand out – to be not just competent, but *effective* – I'm going to walk you through the process of preparing your talk, the audience, and even the room you'll be working with. By the end of the process, you'll be ready to present in a way that moves others to action.

POWER isn't about

presentation tips...

it's a peek behind the

curtain of professional-speaking secrets.

CHAPTER THREE

The 5 Power Presentation Steps

I'm fond of using acronyms as teaching tools. They help take complex processes and break them down into something that's easily mastered and memorized. With that in mind, let's take a look at what POWER stands for:

P – Prepare for the Meeting
O – Open the Meeting
W – Win Attention
E – Entertain and Educate
R – Review for Action

The POWER acronym is a handy way to remember what's important, as well as keeping everything in a natural order. Remember that the point isn't just to make you a great speaker, but to help you use that skill to achieve your professional goals. You want to sell, educate, or persuade

– not simply entertain the audience. So it follows that every step should build toward that goal, and that's exactly how the system is designed. Here's how you do it.

Step 1: Prepare for the Meeting

Your presentation should start a long time before you open your mouth. The moment you're asked to speak to a group, a few questions should come to mind: Who will be in the audience? What do I need to convey to them? How long will I have? The answers will become the backbone of what you're going to say.

Prepare Yourself Mentally

Naturally, the first thing you'll want to do is decide what you're going to say. This is perhaps the most difficult part of the POWER process, but also the one that will pay the biggest dividends. In a one-on-one situation with a client or colleague, you can probably get away with pausing to dig up a note or file, but with a room full of listeners you won't have a similar opportunity. So, it's important that you have your ideas mapped out ahead of time. Besides, preparation is the single best way to cut down on the anxiety that many of us feel when we're going to speak in public.

If you feel like planning your speech is a bit overwhelming, try an old trick I picked up while giving my first few presentations. First, you pull out a piece of paper and write down the number of minutes you will have for your speech. Once you've done that, think of the first thing you'll have to do – probably introduce yourself and the topic of your presentation. Figure out how long that's going to take, subtract it from the total number of minutes, and then start at the next point, usually two or three minutes later. Now, you just have the next minute or two to worry about, not a whole speech.

By breaking your presentation into smaller steps this way, you can turn each piece into something that's more manageable. You never have to map out your presentation; just think of what you want to say for the next ninety seconds or so. Once you've planned your speech this way, you can easily go back and decide what parts to move, reword, add to, or eliminate.

Organize the Agenda, Equipment, and Meeting Room

This is one of the most overlooked parts of the preparation process, but one that you shouldn't skip. Knowing your room, and preparing it as best as you can, can help you set the stage for success – literally and figuratively.

The first thing you'll want to do is simply see where you'll be presenting and get a feel for the space. This is an old trick used not only by speakers, but also comedians, stage actors, and other live performers. There's nothing complicated to the technique; you just never want to have to walk in and deliver in a 'new' room that you don't know. Rather, you should take a few moments to get comfortable in the space, see where everything is, and imagine yourself doing well. As simple as this sounds, you would be amazed at how it can calm your nerves and help you to do your best.

It's also a good idea to run a quick check through the technical components of your presentation. Does your laptop work with the projector, if you're using these? Are all of the outlets functional? What about the sound system? Five minutes spent being sure that everything works can save you a ton of effort and embarrassment later.

Next, you'll want to see how the tables and/or chairs are set up. You might not have a lot of control over how people will be seated for your presentation, but at least you can be aware of how the space is arranged. Will everyone be able to see you? Are there certain places where it's hard to hear? Will the room be set up classroom style, with everyone facing you, or in round tables that encourage group participation? These are all things you'll want to know before it's time to start talking.

And finally, give a quick check to the temperature and lighting. I've found over the years that sixty-eight to seventy degrees is ideal. Any cooler than that, and your audience might be distracted by a chill; go much warmer, and you run the risk of having them be drowsy. This applies to the lighting as well. I've found that brighter is better, within reason. Lots of presenters like to dim the lights so they can use lots of slides or projections, but there's just too much temptation for people's minds to wander in a dark room.

A properly "tuned" room can give you a leg up in holding your audience's attention. Be sure to arrive early enough to get a feel for it and tweak it to your advantage.

Build Pre-Presentation Enthusiasm

This is another point that is often missed by hopeful business presenters. Whether it's four people or four hundred, your audience is made up of individuals. Those people can be strangers, acquaintances, or friends. Obviously, the more of them you have on your side, the easier time you're going to have.

To that end, get to know as many people as possible before you get up to deal with them as a group. Walk around prior to your presentation and introduce yourself. Meet the attendees and let them know that you appreciate their time. Put them on your side. When your time begins, they'll pay you back by greeting you more enthusiastically and giving you more of their attention than they might if they didn't have any connection to you.

Getting the opportunity to meet people is just one more reason to show up early and prepared. Instead of having to check your computer, or the sound and lights, you can take advantage of the chance to make a connection with your audience. It will make you more comfortable, and put them in a frame of mind to help you succeed.

Step 2: Open the Meeting

Once the time for your presentation has arrived, all your hard work and preparation will pay off. And the easiest way to ensure a smooth ride is to start off well.

Offer Your Credentials (Formally or Informally)

People like experts. That is, they want to hear from men and women that know more about a subject than they do. So it's important that you position yourself as an authority on your topic – or at least as someone who has some interesting viewpoints – right at the start. How do you do that? Ideally, you get someone else to do it for you.

What others say about you speaks more loudly than anything you can say about yourself. The same principle applies here, so whenever possible, get someone respected to introduce you in a way that emphasizes your credibility. It could be as simple as having a senior executive start you off with something like, "Hi everybody. This is Joe Junior Manager, and he's got some great ideas on how we might be able to make some more money this year."

If possible, get them to offer more about you, your background and education, or how they came to know you. The more they say to build you up, the easier time you'll have, because they're keying the audience that what you're saying is important. In fact, it's not a bad idea to prepare a short formal introduction and ask your host if he or she wouldn't mind reading it.

There will be times, however, when you either won't have someone to introduce you, or they'll be unable or unwilling to do so. In that case, you'll need to introduce yourself informally. Usually, the best strategy in this case is to simply state the same highlights that would have been in your formal introduction. For instance, you might say something like, "Good morning everybody and thanks for having me here. I know some of you might not know me, but I'm a quality control specialist with Gigantic Solution Company and I've been working on the problem of widget fatigue for more than fifteen years. What I'd like to talk with you about today is..." This kind of opening isn't as strong as a formal introduction by a third party, but it will at least give you a chance to offer your credentials to the audience and give them a reason to listen.

Enthusiastically Connect With Your Audience

As you begin, do so with some energy. Use your enthusiasm to draw people in. Your presentation should reflect the feeling that you have some things you want to share with the group. You might be doing most of the speaking, but you should all be in the room together. As I like to say, "Presenting is something you do with the audience, not too them." That's more than just a cute idea; it's a reminder that an excited, energetic speaker will find their feelings reflected in the audience ... and so will a speaker who is disinterested or apprehensive.

Involve the audience with eye contact, or ask questions so they can give you feedback. Move around, so you're facing different people at different times. If you know some of the names of your attendees, use them. The point is to do whatever you can to keep things interactive as you're making your points. This will help you keep things interesting on both sides.

Another good way to keep up a positive give-and-take is by using the space. I had the chance to spend the day with a stage actor once, and he gave me a helpful tip that I've carried with me since. As presenters, our space extends as far and wide as the room itself. The other people aren't simply passive objects – they're the rest of our cast. Learn to think of them in that light, and you'll be able to avoid the amateur mistake of hiding behind the safety of a lectern, or only noticing the people in the front row.

Open With a Warm-Up Story

One of the biggest challenges for inexperienced presenters is that they don't know how to get started. Even with a prepared outline, they get nervous about what should come after the introduction. How can they transition smoothly through their material while still grabbing the listeners' attention?

Launching straight into their presentation is not a good way. For one thing, it puts a lot of pressure on the speaker to be interesting, not to mention to know their material inside-out, right away. And besides, it often takes a couple of minutes for attendees to shift their thinking from whatever was preoccupying their minds before the presentation into the matter at hand.

A better, and time-honored, method is to begin with a warm-up story. It doesn't need to be anything elaborate, just something that pertains to you, your audience, or the issue at hand, and that ties them together in a way that makes your audience want to hear you out.

Here's a warm-up story I use pretty frequently in my own presentations:

Several years ago, before my son entered high school, my wife and I enrolled him in a weekend football camp. I thought the activity, which was being led by a few former pro players, might be a good chance for him to meet some new friends and have a little bit of fun. Plus, there was always the chance that he might pick up something that would help him be a better player.

And so it was no surprise when he came home that Saturday full of enthusiasm. He wanted to show me all the things he had learned over the last couple of days. Being that it was a perfect fall afternoon, I decided to head out to the backyard and throw the pigskin around with him for a bit.

Well, we weren't five minutes into tossing it back and forth before he came running up to me to let me know I wasn't holding the football the right way. Being that I had been playing and watching the game roughly a couple of decades longer than he'd been alive, I laughed off the suggestion.

Eventually though, after he'd mentioned it a few times, I decided to humor him. After all, I was the one who'd spent the money to send him to camp, and I wanted him to feel good about what he had practiced. And so I stood patiently while he explained where my hand should go over the football, and how I could draw back my arm to throw a more consistent spiral.

That's when a funny thing happened... I tried it a couple times and realized he was right. But taking my son's advice, I actually learned a better way to throw a football – more than twenty years after I'd started doing it.

I tell you this story because I think it's a pretty good analogy for what we're going to be talking about today. You're all good at your jobs already, and you probably have ways of doing things that have worked for many years. But just because things are working doesn't mean that there might not be a few things you can pick up that will make your job a little bit easier. I hope you'll give me just a little bit of your time and attention so I can tell you what I've learned about...

This story is one of my favorites because it gives me a good connection with my audience – most people can relate to the situation I was in with my son – but also because it gives them an implicit reason to hear me out. I'm making the point that I don't necessarily know everything, but there still might be value in my presentation.

Like many of these steps, the warm-up story serves a dual purpose. On the one hand, it transitions the audience from your introduction – along with many of the thoughts that might still be lingering in their minds – into the presentation. But it also helps to settle you into what you're doing. After all, stories are the easy part. You don't have to relate heavy facts or figures, just talk about something that happened. And there's not much risk that you'll forget anything, because it's your story!

While you don't have to have anything written out word-for-word, it's a good idea to use a warm-up story to win the audience over. They'll appreciate the transition, and you might too.

Step 3: Win Attention

Once you've told your warm-up story, it's time to get down to the main topic of your presentation, and to do it in a way that locks the room into what you're saying. If you're going to be effective as a presenter – if you're going to motivate your listeners to action – you'll want to be sure to lock in the audience's attention.

Address the Needs of the Group

You'll want to open up by speaking to the group's needs, and at the same time answering the key question in their minds: *why are you there talking to them, and why should they care?* This could be as simple as saying, "I'm here today because your company has been looking at some new policies," or some other clearly-stated purpose. If you've been following The 5 POWER Presentation Steps up to this point, the audience should like and trust you. You reward that confidence by giving them a reason to listen.

Use the Questioning Technique to Create Interest in Your Message

An excellent technique for focusing your group is to ask a series of questions that point to your presentation topic. Using a set of three that all require "yes" or "no" answers is especially effective. For example, you might follow your introduction and warm-up story with something like this: "I'm here today because you've been interested in upgrading your production equipment. But before I begin, would it be okay with you if I asked you a few questions? Would you like to have a quieter production floor? Could you use equipment that was more energy efficient and environmentally friendly? Do you want to work with the highest-quality tools available?"

By giving the audience three things that they agree with, you've mentally prepared them to hear you out in order to find out how they can enjoy these benefits. Even though we're presenting, we're back to the basics of showmanship. First, you grab their attention, and then you deliver your message.

Get Your Audience Involved in the Presentation

Again, it's important to remember that you should always be presenting *with* your group, never at them. To this end, keep them involved in what you're doing. Ask questions that they can answer, use handouts and demos that can be passed around the room, or at the very least, get them to raise their hands or move around. Anything that keeps them engaged in the process makes it more interesting, and more effective.

Step 4: Entertain and Educate

Ask anyone to think back to their favorite professor, and they'll probably name someone who was as much an entertainer as they were a teacher. This trait of human nature – that we love to be joked with and thrilled – is an effective presentation tool. But it also requires work. We live in a society that has been spoiled for entertainment. You're never farther away than your computer, television, or even cell phone from being able to see something dazzling. Perhaps this is why our attention span for things that don't interest us has shrunk so much. Be prepared to excite your audience a bit and make it easy for them to follow you.

Illustrate Your Message Using Showmanship

This goes back to your quotes, stories, and humor. In my seminars, I teach a number of advanced techniques that presenters can use to add drama using their voice and body language. Because these methods are difficult to show in a book, let me just say that when you speak in public, you shouldn't leave your body at home. You don't have to make your group feel like they're watching a three-ring circus, but mix it up a little.

Creatively Use Any Tools Available to Support Your Message

Back when I was learning to present, flip charts and handouts were the most popular ways to add something more to your talk. More recently, software packages like PowerPoint and Keynote have made it easier than ever to add elements like graphics, music, and even video clips to your presentation. If you're going to be using these tools, and I definitely recommend that you try them, take a bit of time to learn to utilize them effectively. Done well, they can add a little extra spice to what you're saying.

Used poorly, they can distract from your message and your credibility.

And speaking of spices, treat these extras like you would a powerful chili pepper. In other words, a little goes a long way. They should accent a strong message, not serve as a substitute. Too much of a computerized gimmick doesn't just bore your attendees – it ruins their appetite. Remember that your audience came to see and hear you, not your laptop.

Encourage Feedback During Your Presentation

You'll want to check in with your audience from time to time and be sure they're following along. Stop now and then to ask little questions like, "Wouldn't you all agree?" or "Doesn't that make sense?" Don't be afraid to take the group's temperature from time to time. It's important that they follow you and understand what you're saying before you move into the final part of your presentation – reviewing your key points and moving them to take action.

Step 5: Review for Action

Within all of these tips, it might be tempting to think that putting on a good show is more important than your message. And while it's true that you'll need to entertain a bit if you want to succeed as a presenter, don't lose sight of what that success should mean: moving others to take action. With that in mind, let's take a look at how we wrap up the talk and turn your excited audience members into persuaded individuals.

Review Key Points of Your Message

After you've wrapped up the body of your message, go back over the highlights. This gives you the opportunity not only to emphasize certain points, but also to make them more memorable in the minds of your attendees. Boil your talk back down to five or fewer critical items that you want attendees to hold on to – usually the most important benefits of your proposal – and repeat them now.

Ask Attendees if They Found the Information Helpful

You should already know the answer to this, but it's another quick question that allows you to gauge how well you've won over the attendees. If they enthusiastically agree that hearing you out has been a good use of their time, then you know you've made a convincing case. If they're not as quick to offer positive feedback, then you might want to try to take a moment and return to a key message. It's absolutely critical that you leave the audience feeling like they've gotten value for their attention before you ask them to go further.

Request Positive Action

If you've followed The 5 POWER Presentation Steps, the audience should be right where you want them. They know all about you and your background. What's more, they trust you and the information you've presented, and see what you're recommending as a valuable solution to their problems. Now, you want to use that momentum to flow toward some action. You shouldn't have to come on very strong to make this happen. Something as simple as this will usually do the trick: *"Now might be the time for us to make some changes. If you feel, as I do – that it's time to try something new – I'm ready to implement the plan we talked about today and start moving forward immediately."*

The most important thing is that you ask them to do exactly what you want them to do. Do you want them to approve your new budget, name you as head of a division, or place a big order? Whatever it is, have a plan to take advantage of the excitement and energy that will come out of your preparation and hard work, and make it as easy as possible for your attendees to take the next natural step.

If it's your first time presenting, you might just be surprised at how willing people are to follow your recommendations. Becoming a strong business presenter takes a lot of work, but it can have an enormous impact on your career. Few things in this world are as persuasive as having someone stand before you and confidently deliver their case. Great presentations don't just sell products and persuade others to your point of view; they also help us choose our leaders and examine the ways we think about ourselves and our future.

I invite you to go back through this chapter as many times as you need, to learn The 5 POWER Presentation steps thoroughly. They might seem overwhelming at first, but once you master the pieces and put them together into a killer presentation, you'll be able to do something that all of your colleagues will see, but few of them can match.

You have to bring your
passion and energy.
The last thing the world needs
is another bored person
working hard to bore the rest of us.

CHAPTER FOUR

Getting the Most out of Power

Several years ago, I was hired by a company to come in and teach The 5 POWER Presentation Steps to members of their sales staff and management team. It was a good group, and they took lots of notes, so it didn't surprise me when a young man approached me shortly after I'd finished speaking. But contrary to what I had expected, he didn't have any questions about the best way to refine his presentation or connect with an audience. Instead, he wanted to know why I wasn't looking out for my own interests.

"You're giving everything away," he started off by saying. "With what you just told us, anyone in this room could practice and become a great speaker. Suppose lots of people decided to do that... then what would happen to your business?"

I bring this up because the young men was half right; it took me years upon years to learn the simple methods and techniques outlined in a short book. Anyone reading it could master The 5 POWER Presentation Steps and go on to become my competition.

But you know what? They won't. I know this for the same reason I know that you can put these tools into action and use them to rise head and shoulders above your peers: because becoming a powerful speaker is hard work. It doesn't happen overnight, and there aren't many ways to shorten the learning curve. If you're going to be any good, then you'd better be prepared to practice giving your presentation hundreds of times, refining it step-by-step each time it comes out of your mouth.

Only then, after you've made the dozens of mistakes that we all inevitably make, and had a few speeches go really, really badly, could you understand what it takes to make speaking a big part of your career. I've purposely designed the POWER program to be straightforward. Anyone can follow its steps and put together an impactful business presentation. But while it can help you with the first two ingredients for a top-tier speech – material and showmanship – there are no shortcuts to the third: *your persona.*

Powerful speakers and presenters weren't born that way. It takes a long time to develop a presence and confidence on stage that literally draws listeners in. I've been a professional presenter, in one form or another, for more than 20 years, and I'm still learning every week.

Realizing that few of you probably aspire to go on to become professional speakers, why do I bother to mention all of this? Because, as with most endeavors, there's room at the top. The fact that effective presenting takes some dedication means that most people aren't ever going to attempt it. If you can stick with it, even through the setbacks and frustrations I just mentioned, you are going to quickly surpass your peers and competition.

I have one friend and colleague who became a leader within his industry by speaking at industry functions. In just a short time, his career took off in directions he never could have anticipated. He's now the head of a major association – something that would have been unthinkable to him ten years ago. And why? Because he learned to express his thoughts and opinions in a way that caused other people to take action. You can do the same.

But I need to be upfront in telling you that it isn't as easy as it looks. Like I said, I've been doing this for quite a while and I can still say that I'm figuring it out. So, I'd like to devote the rest of this chapter to a few tips that can help you reduce the amount of time it will take for you to become a world-class business presenter.

Learn The 5 POWER Presentation Steps Inside-Out

Don't think I'm advocating this just because I came up with the system. Everything you've read in these short pages is a distilled version of the knowledge and experience that it took me decades to figure out. By following my roadmap, you can skip a lot of the most frustrating dead ends. Plus, knowing how to put an effective presentation together, and focusing on those steps, takes a great deal of fear and anxiety out of the speaking process. As long as you remain focused on the points I've outlined, your speeches are going to be at least better than average.

POWER isn't a simplified method for public speaking – it's what you would develop by studying this business on your own for a very long time. I hope you'll devote some time to seeing how it works. It won't just save you from inventing the wheel; it will keep you from wasting years and developing bad habits.

Take every chance you get to speak in public

In order to become a superior presenter, you need to learn to feel confident and relaxed in front of groups. The only way I know to accomplish that is with a lot of practice. Every speech is hard when you're giving it for the first time; most are very easy when you're giving them for the thousandth time. Somewhere along the way, a piece of magic happens, and everything starts to sink in. Your movements, tone of voice, and emotional connection with the audience all improve dramatically.

It takes a bit of time on stage to develop that, though, so make sure to start speaking early and often.

Learn about software and other tools

When I got started, pie charts were cutting-edge. Now, there are not only hundreds of different visual aids you can use, but even interactive controllers that allow audience members to ask questions, answer polls, and otherwise give feedback throughout your presentation. To those developments, you could also add changes in lighting, sound, and staging to the features presenters can take advantage of now.

Any of these can become an asset, or just a crutch. The difference, obviously, is in how you use them. But you can't use any tool effectively until you understand it. With that in mind, never stop trying new pieces of technology, and never rely on any one or two to make or break your presentation. For all of the great things we can do these days, hard drives still fail, microphones still cut out, and handheld electronics still run out of batteries. Use any tool you have at your disposal to make your presentation more effective, but never let any of them become the focus of your speech.

Strive for constant improvement

Earlier, I mentioned that it's not a bad idea to take some classes on humor if you're serious about giving high-impact presentations, and I'll repeat that suggestion again. In fact, there are a number of different courses and groups that can help you give stronger speeches, from Toastmasters meetings to weekend seminars on storytelling and body language. These are not only great options because they increase your skill set, but also because they keep you from getting stale.

The worst trouble in presenting doesn't usually come from the first few talks when you feel like you're doing terribly; you might be bad, but audiences will give you credit for trying. The bigger problem is when you get too comfortable. Anybody can go through the motions, but the moment you start getting lazy, the old routines don't work as well anymore. Audiences can feel it when you're phoning it in, so it's crucial that you continue growing as a presenter and keep things fresh.

Remember that passion is persuasive

A lot of people struggle to identify what it is that makes a specific presentation so compelling. I studied the riddle for years: two people can give nearly identical talks, hit the same high notes, carry themselves well, and even tell similar jokes or stories. And yet, one will be a hit and the other won't. Eventually, I noticed that the difference is almost always in passion and energy. Listeners can tell which one cares the most, and they respond to that.

If you feel like you can't give a presentation with any enthusiasm, don't. The last thing the world needs is another bored person working hard to bore the rest of us. There's a simple formula for success on any stage: bring your excitement to every speech you give, or don't open your mouth at all.

The 5 POWER Presentation Steps aren't so much about better public speaking as they are about opening up possibilities for your career. As you look back through them, I hope you'll remember that the parts that seem overwhelming now will become routine later. Like everything else in your life, becoming a great speaker just takes practice and perseverance. But unlike most other things you can work at, it will take you to heights you never thought you'd reach.

Good luck, and I look forward to hearing your presentation soon.

Carl Henry is a sales educator, keynote speaker and corporate consultant. During the course of his own successful career, he developed The MODERN Sales System, which he has been sharing with companies and associations around the world for many years.

A Certified Speaking Professional and a member of the National Speakers Association, Carl teaches essential sales skills with humor, insight and personal experience. Hundreds of companies throughout a diverse range of industries have used his highly-acclaimed seminars to educate and inspire their sales teams.

Carl's other books include The MODERN Sales System, 15 Hot Tips That Will Supercharge Your Sales Career, The PEOPLE Approach to Customer Service, Sell Something Everyday, 52 Things Every Sales Manager Needs to Know, and High Energy Sales Thoughts.

He currently lives in Charlotte, North Carolina.

To order additional copies of this book, or find out about Carl's seminars contact him at:

Henry Associates
704-847-7390
9430 Valley Road Charlotte, NC 28270
chenry@carlhenry.com
www.carlhenry.com

To order additional copies of this book contact:

Henry Associates
704-847-7390
9430 Valley Road Charlotte, NC 28270
chenry@carlhenry.com
www.carlhenry.com

www.ingramcontent.com/pod-product-compliance
Lightning Source LLC
LaVergne TN
LVHW010545100826
845148LV00013B/2607

* 9 7 8 0 9 8 1 7 9 1 5 4 8 *